The Story of…

THE RACE TO THE
SOUTH POLE

Nick Sa

ticktock

Robert Falcon Scott: *(1868-1912): Scott was an officer in the Royal Naval and an Antarctic explorer. Despite a lack of polar experience, he led an expedition to the South Pole in the ship* Discovery *(1901-3). This failed to reach the Pole, so in June 1910 he set off again, this time on the ship* Terra Nova. *Tragically, Scott and his five-man team died in March 1912, while returning from the Pole in terrible weather conditions. Scott's bravery and endurance made him a national hero.*

Roald Engelbregth Gravning Amundsen: *(1872-1928): Amundsen was a Norwegian polar explorer. He made headlines when he crossed the Northwest Passage linking the Atlantic and Pacific oceans. Amundsen planned to reach the North Pole, but after Robert Peary's American team got there first, he set out for Antarctica instead. His five-man team raced Scott to the South Pole, helped by better planning and their use of dogs and skis. Amundsen died when his plane crashed into Arctic waters in June 1928.*

Ernest Shackleton: *(1874-1922): Born in Ireland, Shackleton took part in Scott's 1901-3 Discovery Expedition. Between 1907-9, he organised and led the British National Antarctic Expedition, which came within 180 km of the South Pole. In his 1914 expedition to cross the Antarctic, his ship* Endurance *was crushed in the ice. He sailed, in a small boat, to get help in a remarkable journey across the South Atlantic Ocean. He died of a heart attack, attempting to sail around the Antarctic.*

Fridtjof Nansen: *(1861-1930): Nansen was a famous Norwegian explorer, scientist and diplomat. He first made his name with an expedition crossing Greenland on skis in 1888. In 1893, he sailed to the Arctic in the* Fram, *a ship later used by Amundsen. This journey took three years and was the first voyage to cross the Arctic Ocean. In 1922, he was awarded a Nobel Peace Prize for his work in helping war prisoners and refugees after the First W*~~orld War~~

Lawrence Oates: *(1880-19..)* ... *Boer War in South Africa. In* ... *partly due to his knowledge of* ... *man team to travel the final l* ... *increasingly weak. He sacrific* ...

Olav Bjaaland: *(1873- 196..)* ... *member of Amundsen's five-m..* ... *skilled carpenter who modifie..* ... *He later set up a ski factory a..*

WORCESTERSHIRE COUNTY COUNCIL	
549	
Bertrams	25.11.06
J919.89	£5.99
WS	

Copyright © ticktock Entertainment Ltd. 2006
First published in Great Britain in 2006 by ticktock Media Ltd.,
Unit 2, Orchard Business Centre, North Farm Road, Tunbridge Wells, Kent, TN2 3XF
ISBN 1 84696 044 4
Printed in China
A CIP catalogue record for this book is available from the British Library.

CONTENTS

TO THE ENDS OF THE EARTH

The year is 1911. Blinded by blizzards, two groups of explorers struggle over a harsh, icy landscape. One group is led by Norwegian explorer Roald Amundsen, the other by Captain Robert Falcon Scott, a British naval officer.

Scott's team faced particularly harsh weather conditions.

Amundsen beat Scott and was the first to reach the South Pole.

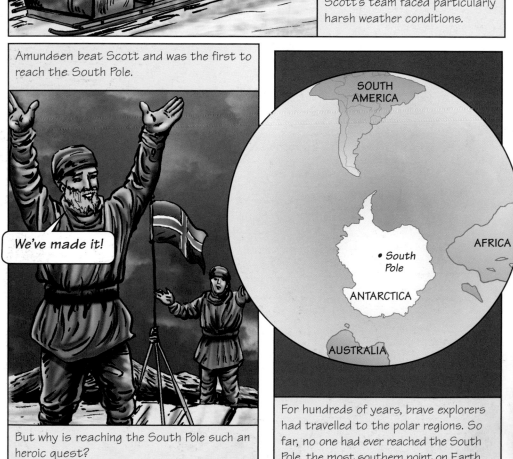

But why is reaching the South Pole such an heroic quest?

For hundreds of years, brave explorers had travelled to the polar regions. So far, no one had ever reached the South Pole, the most southern point on Earth.

The sea voyage to Antarctica takes several weeks. To reach the South Pole means a 2,400 km trek through icy mountains. Temperatures drop to -84°C in winter and fierce winds lash the landscape.

In 330 BC, the Greek explorer Pytheas crossed the Arctic Circle and reached the Arctic pack ice. His crew were the first people to see the Midnight Sun.

The Sun never sets in this strange land.

A thousand years later, Vikings sailed in Arctic waters. These fierce warriors from Norway and Denmark sailed across the Atlantic in their longships.

Look for seals. We are running short of food!

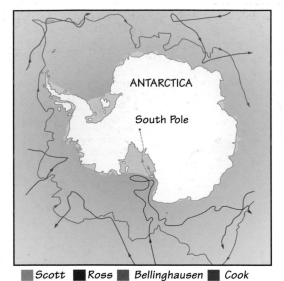

In 1739, Captain Jean-Baptiste Bouvet tried to claim the undiscovered "South Land" for France. He reached Bouvet Island, 1,600 km north of Antarctica.

Many explorers have tried to reach the South Pole, here are some of their routes.

Captain Cook came within a day's sail of the coastline. Unfortunately heavy pack ice forced him to turn back.

In January 1773, Englishman Captain James Cook and his crew sailed around Antarctica, without ever seeing it!

In 1820, Thaddeus von Bellinghausen of Russia led the first expedition to see the Antarctic coastline, beating an English ship by only a few days.

In 1827, Captain William Parry led a failed expedition to the North Pole. The race to the Poles had begun!

In 1841, Englishman James Clark Ross found a quicker route to the South Pole.

He also discovered the Ross Ice Shelf and the smoking volcano, Mount Erebus.

Shortly after, in 1845, John Franklin led an expedition to find a route through the ice from the Atlantic to the Pacific.

Franklin and 128 of his men died from starvation, cold and disease. Franklin still became a hero, and the inspiration for two young boys named Robert Scott and Roald Amundsen. Our story really starts here…

FAST FACT Local Inuit peoples knew how to survive in the icy environment that killed Franklin. Later polar explorers copied methods used by the Inuits, such as using snowshoes.

YOUNG EXPLORERS

Roald Amundsen and Robert Scott developed a passion for exploration early in life. They ended up racing each other to the South Pole.

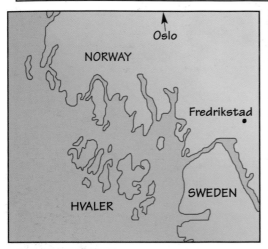

Roald Amundsen was born on 16th July, 1872, into a family of sailors and shipbuilders from the islands of Hvaler, in Norway.

Roald grew up in Christiania (now Oslo). As a boy he loved playing outdoors. Skiing was very popular in Norway and Roald learned to ski as soon as he could walk.

Hurry up, Eric, I'm in training.

Wait for me — you're too fast!

Old Eric, a shipbuilder who worked for Roald's father, taught Roald and his brothers about boats and sailing.

Why are you so interested in boats, Roald?

One day I'm going to be an explorer!

Roald always slept with the window open, even during the freezing Norwegian winters.

Leaving the window open will make me tough!

Roald's father wanted him to be a doctor. But Roald wanted to be like Nansen, the famous Norwegian explorer.

Roald Amundsen grew into a tall, strong boy with fair hair and deep blue eyes. He was obsessed with being fit and tough.

You're the last of the Vikings, Roald!

'72... 73...74... Gasp!

In 1893, Amundsen saw Nansen's new ship, the Fram, set sail from Christiania. He was determined to go on his own polar expedition.

One day that will be me heading for the Poles.

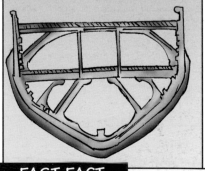

FAST FACT The Fram had a revolutionary design. The ship was shaped like a saucer, so that it could be lifted above floating ice, rather than crushed by it.

As part of his polar training, Amundsen did long cross-country skiing trips in the mountains with his friend Laurentius Urdahl.

I'm exhausted. Let's camp near here.

Come on. Let's do a few more kilometres.

FAST FACT On one ski trip Amundsen almost lost his fingers from frostbite. Frostbite is skin damage caused by extreme cold.

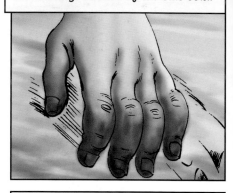

In 1896, Amundsen joined his first Antarctic expedition.

Welcome aboard the Belgica, Mr Amundsen.

Amundsen fell in love with the icy landscape. He also learned a great deal from experienced explorers on the expedition.

It's deadly, too. You never know when a blizzard will hit.

It's so quiet and beautiful out here.

In 1903, Amundsen first made the headlines when he led an expedition in a 20-metre fishing boat through the Northwest Passage. This was the same journey that had killed one of his hero's, John Franklin.

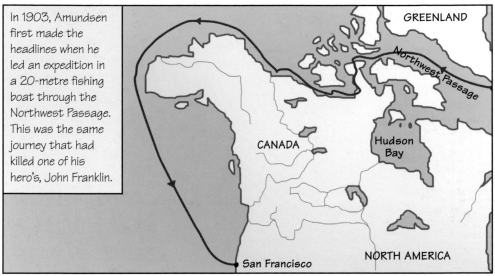

GREENLAND

Northwest Passage

CANADA

Hudson Bay

NORTH AMERICA

San Francisco

The journey took three years to complete. During the winters, the ship was trapped in the ice.

We can't go any further. The ice is too thick.

Amundsen tried to reach the North Pole on foot, but failed.

Inuit hunters showed Amundsen how to dress warmly in loose furs, how to drive dog sledges and other survival skills.

These dogs will keep running for hours!

Back home, in Norway, Amundsen became a hero.

Robert Falcon Scott was born on 6th June, 1868. He grew up near the naval dockyards in Plymouth, England.

Nicknamed Con by his family, Scott was a sickly child who did not go to school until he was 8 years old.

You need to rest, Con.

At 13, Con was sent into the Royal Navy by his father. Two years later, he joined his first ship. It was a tough, brutal life. Even in rough seas, young officers worked in the rigging 40 metres above deck.

Hurry up, Scott. The storm is getting stronger.

For 10 years, Scott was a junior officer sailing all over the world. Then, in 1894, Scott's father became bankrupt. He died four years later, as did Scott's brother.

My family depends on me. I need a promotion to get more money.

Then, by chance, Scott met Sir Clements Markham, who was organising a British Antarctic Expedition.

Britain needs to get there first!

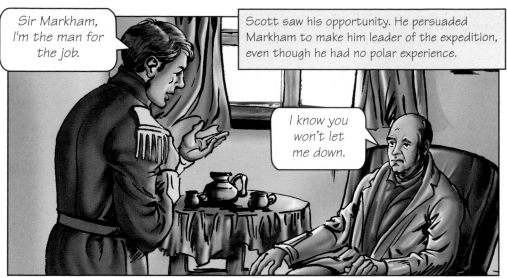

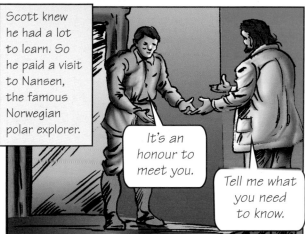

Over the next year, Scott made detailed plans and picked his crew. This included Ernest Shackleton, who later became a famous polar explorer. Meanwhile a new ship, HMS Discovery, was being built for the expedition.

Scott's first British Antarctic Expedition set off from England in July 1901. It reached Antarctica in early 1902, sailing along the coast past the area explored by Ross.

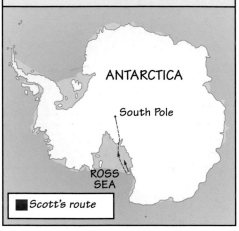

ANTARCTICA

South Pole

ROSS SEA

Scott's route

FAST FACT Scott and Shackleton went up in a hot air balloon on 4 February, 1902, to get an overview of the Antarctic expedition area. But the balloon sprung a leak, so it wasn't used again.

A hut was built on Ross Island for storage and work space.

I'll get the dogs ready.

We should do some practice sledge runs.

In December 1902, Scott headed for the South Pole with Shackleton and Wilson. In 93 days they travelled over 1,500 km but bad weather, hunger, frostbite and exhaustion forced them to turn back. The following year Scott explored Victoria Land with Lashly and Evans, but blizzards again forced them to head for home.

The dogs are suffering badly.

This blizzard is going to bury us alive!

On their way back, Scott and Evans fell into a deep crevasse.

Scott and Evans were left dangling with blue walls of ice on either side and a dark chasm below them.

Amazingly, Scott swung his feet around and gripped the wall with his crampons. Using the last of his strength, Scott climbed out safely.

Then, Lashly pulled Evans up.

Back in England, Scott was made Captain and he wrote a popular book, "The Voyage of the Discovery". By early 1907, he was already thinking about another Antarctic expedition.

THE RACE BEGINS

So far, neither the North or South Pole had been reached. At this point, Scott and Amundsen's attentions were focused on different Poles. Amundsen on the North, and Scott on the South. All that was about to change.

Meanwhile, on 6th April, 1909, two Americans, Robert Peary and Matthew Henson claimed to have reached the North Pole. They were helped by a team of 24 Inuits and 130 dogs.

At last! We've done it after 18 years and 6 attempts!

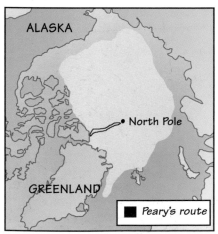

ALASKA

• North Pole

GREENLAND

■ Peary's route

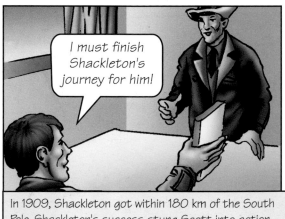

I must finish Shackleton's journey for him!

In 1909, Shackleton got within 180 km of the South Pole. Shackleton's success stung Scott into action.

Amundsen had also been planning to reach the North Pole. He had already asked Nansen for help.

Can I borrow the Fram?

You'll have to persuade the government!

Amundsen got the Fram and 75,000 kroner from the Norwegian government. Then, just three months before he was due to set off...

I don't believe it! Peary's got there first.

Now I'll have to beat Scott to the South Pole!

By August 1910, Amundsen was ready to lead his own expedition to the South Pole. But all the world thought he was headed in the opposite direction!

I can't risk telling anyone, not even Nansen.

Scott was busy with his own preparations. Early in March 1910, he went to Norway to test the motor sledges for his expedition.

We will probably need to use animals as well.

Nansen introduced an expert skier, Tryggve Gran, to Scott.

Let me show you how easy it is on skis!

While in Norway, Scott tried to meet Amundsen. But Amundsen wanted to keep his plans secret.

May I speak to Mr Amundsen?

Tell him I'm not here.

The Navy let Scott pick his own crew. Lieutenant Teddy Evans was put in charge of Scott's ship, the *Terra Nova*.

You'll have to work fast. We set sail in June.

8,000 men volunteered to go on the expedition. Scott chose 24 to go with him.

Be warned. This is going to a be a long, hard journey.

The crew included several scientists, among them experts in biology, geology and meteorology. Scott wanted to be sure that he had the best team.

There is so much we don't know about the Antarctic.

Captain Oates was put in charge of the ponies bought in Siberia, Russia.

Scott also bought a few teams of sledge dogs. But after his bad experiences on the *Discovery Expedition*, he did not trust them.

Back in Norway, Amundsen studied Shackleton's map for the 1909 expedition.

We only need a small team of skiers and dog sledges.

Amundsen ordered new skis, goggles and sealskin clothes from Greenland.

At last, all our equipment is here.

Carpenter Jørgen Stubberud built a winter hut, for the expedition, in Amundsen's garden. It had 11 bunks and a separate room for cooking.

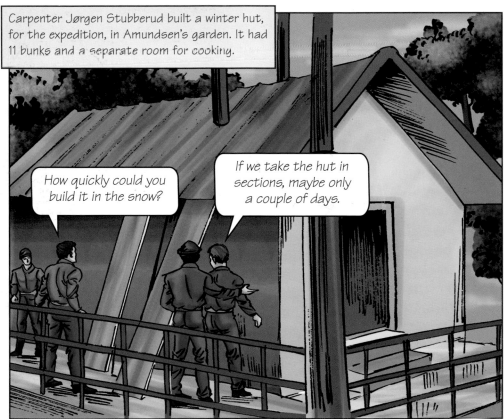

How quickly could you build it in the snow?

If we take the hut in sections, maybe only a couple of days.

Amundsen's men were all good skiers and used to a cold climate. Amundsen included a ski champion, Olav Bjaaland, in his team.

Bravo!

Amundsen believed the trek to the Pole would be a long ski race. He took 2.5 metre skis made from solid wood, to help his team cross deep crevasses.

The ski works like a bridge.

Amundsen did not want his men to pull their own sledges. It was too tiring. Instead he took well-trained dogs, bought in Greenland, to pull them. He also hired two expert dog-handlers, Helmer Hanssen and Sverre Hassel.

Mush! Mush!

FAST FACT   Huskies are dogs that are closely related to wolves. If a dog died it could be fed to the rest of the team, to keep them going.

Scott and Amundsen were each determined to be the first to reach the South Pole. They left for Antarctica within days of each other. Amundsen was the first to leave.

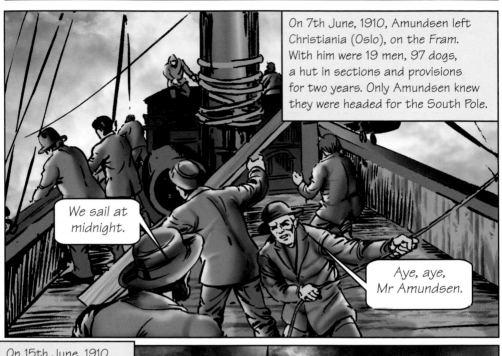

On 7th June, 1910, Amundsen left Christiania (Oslo), on the *Fram*. With him were 19 men, 97 dogs, a hut in sections and provisions for two years. Only Amundsen knew they were headed for the South Pole.

We sail at midnight.

Aye, aye, Mr Amundsen.

On 15th June, 1910, the *Terra Nova* set sail. On board Scott's ship were 65 men, 3 motor sledges, 19 ponies, and 33 dogs. Thousands of people came to cheer them.

Hurrah for Scott!

On 6th September, the Fram docked at Madeira. Amundsen finally told his crew where they were going.

We're heading for the South Pole!

At first, Amundsen's crew were shocked. However, they knew they were better skiers than Scott's party.

We'll race the English!

And we'll get there first.

Amundsen sent a telegram to Scott, who had stopped in Australia for supplies.

Amundsen's going for the South Pole, too!

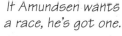

If Amundsen wants a race, he's got one.

On 29th November, 1910, Terra Nova began the final leg of its voyage to the Antarctic. Three days later it was hit by a screaming gale. The storm lasted 36 hours and it nearly sank the ship.

Captain, two of the ponies have been killed.

Mr Evans, we're taking on water fast. The pump is broken!

Arriving at Ross Island in January 1911, Scott found that ice blocked the way to the old hut from the *Discovery Expedition*, so he established a new base camp at Cape Evans, also on Ross Island.

Within two weeks a new hut was built and the stores were brought ashore.

The depot teams were hit by blizzards. The ponies suffered very badly. On one occasion the dogs pounced on a pony and attacked it.

Scott loved to watch the aurora, an amazing natural display of colours that flows across the Poles. Green, purple and blue lights can fill the sky during it.

In the end, the depots were laid. Scott's team got on with their scientific studies. Herbert Ponting took photos of the local wildlife.

On one occasion, Ponting was attacked by killer whales but managed to escape!

Help!

I'd better go out to check on the ponies.

On 23 April, the Sun sank below the horizon. It would not appear again until August. The long Antarctic winter had begun.

The hut was cramped, but there were happy moments. Scott celebrated his 43rd birthday there.

Happy Birthday!

Amundsen also reached Antarctica in January, 1911. He sailed to the Ross Ice Shelf and set up base camp in the Bay of Whales. His camp was 100 km closer to the Pole than Scott's, which was a big advantage.

Look at those giant cliffs!

Bjaaland and Stubberud quickly put up the hut they had tested in Amundsen's garden. Named "Framheim" (home of Fram), this was to be their home for the long winter.

It's time to feed the dogs.

Hurry up, men, it will be dark soon.

Like Scott, Amundsen laid depots before starting the long journey to the Pole. This meant his men would not have to carry supplies for the entire journey.

We'll need this seal meat on the way back.

To lay the depots, Amundsen's men had to travel into unexplored territory in very bad weather. Fortunately, Amundsen's dogs coped well.

FAST FACT Amundsen's men built a warren of snow caves in the ice to provide workshops and even a laundry and toilet, all linked to the main hut.

During the winter, Amundsen's men prepared for the big trek. Bjaaland lightened the sledges by nearly one-third to make them faster.

A light sledge will be easier to pull up the glacier.

We also need to make the cooking equipment lighter.

AGAINST THE ELEMENTS

On October 20, 1911, Amundsen's team of five men, four sledges and 52 dogs set off for the South Pole. They travelled the most direct route possible, going over anything that got in their way. They made good progress, travelling 32 km each day.

On 5 November, they reached their last supply depot. At this point, Amundsen and his team were still 750 km from the Pole.

On 11 November, Amundsen could see mountains in the distance. He named these Queen Maud after the Norwegian Queen. His men began the long climb up the glacier, led by Bjaaland, the ski champion.

Luckily, the weather was good. By 21 November they had reached the summit. The dogs had pulled a tonne of supplies to an altitude of 3,000 metres.

I'm sorry!

South Pole

Amundsen's Route

Shackleton's 1909 Route, followed by Scott's team

Queen Maud Mountains

Queen Alexandra Range

Bay of Whales

At the top, they shot 24 dogs to save supplies. Eighteen dogs would be used in the final push to the Pole.

FAST FACT Amundsen's route was shorter but he took a big risk. He did not know he would find a route through the mountains. Scott followed Shackleton's 1909 route.

Scott and his men set off on 1 November, 1911. His party included two motor sledges and 10 men, each with a pony and sledge. Two others followed with dog sledges. The two motor sledges soon broke down. Amundsen was already 320 km ahead.

Soon the ponies were in trouble, too.

Every 110 km, Scott's party laid new depots. Each contained enough food and fuel for a week, for the return journey.

On 5 December, a fierce blizzard hit Scott's men.

Cold hands and strong winds made it hard to put up tents.

The wind is too strong.

We'll have to wait until the storm is over.

The blizzard kept Scott pinned down for five days, wasting valuable time.

After the blizzard, the ponies could hardly stand. The last five were shot, to be eaten by the team on their return.

FAST FACT Scott was very unlucky with the weather. The extreme cold killed many of his ponies — even their sweat froze onto their sides.

From now on, Scott's men pulled their own sledges. A party of 12, divided into groups, began to haul the sledges up the Beardmore Glacier towards the summit, 3,200 metres above.

Amundsen's men were already at the top, tackling the last difficult obstacle before reaching the South Pole. The "Devil's Ballroom" was a glacier with a thin crust of snow covering a number of dangerous, deep crevasses.

A few days march from the Pole, Amundsen planted a black flag to mark the route for his return.

For Scott's men the real struggle had only just begun. Each man was pulling over 90 kg, while sinking up to his knees in the soft snow.

Keep going, lads!

Blizzards made it impossible to see ahead...

AARRGGHH!

I can't see!

Some of Scott's men suffered from snow-blindness. Others stumbled into crevasses, pulling their sledges down with them. It was slow-going. On 13 December, Scott's men travelled just 6 km in 9 hours.

We can't leave the sledge behind, We need those supplies.

FAST FACT Snow-blindness is a common problem for polar explorers. It is caused by the reflection of bright sunlight from the snow, burning a person's eyes.

Meanwhile, helped by very good weather, Amundsen's team finally reached the South Pole on 14 December, 1911. There was a loud cry of "Halt!" as the sledge meters showed they had arrived at the South Pole. The race was won.

Amundsen's men set up camp. For three days they made calculations to make sure that they really were at the South Pole. They also kept an eye out for Scott.

There's no one else in sight!

They planted the Norwegian flag to show that they had reached the South Pole.

There was a party in the tent that evening and each man shared a little seal meat. Bjaaland pulled out a surprise case of cigars.

What a teast!

Amundsen put up a small tent, with a message inside for Scott, and a letter for the Norwegian King Haakon.

Amundsen was keen to get back to base camp and spread the news. Little did he know that Scott was almost 500 km behind.

We need to tell the world that we got here first.

FAST FACT Trekking across the snow is hard work at high altitude. Amundsen's men spent 16 hours a day in their sleeping bags, conserving their energy.

Down on the Beardmore Glacier, things were getting easier for Scott's men and they were making better progress.

On 3 January, Scott chose four men to continue with him to the Pole and instructed the other three to return.

There was no sign of the Norwegians.

On 13 January Scott's team began the final leg to the South Pole, in better spirits.

Then one foggy morning...

What's that over there?

Amundsen got here first!

On 16 January, Scott's team came across Amundsen's black flag and the remains of his camp. They knew the race was lost.

Scott felt responsible...

I've let everyone down...

FAST FACT From the time that the *Terra Nova* reached New Zealand, Scott wrote down his thoughts and feelings in 12 notebooks. He was a very good writer and the diary remains a gripping read.

THE RACE ENDS

Scott reached the South Pole on 17 January, 1912. He found Amundsen's tent and note – they had arrived 33 days earlier. Scott planted the Union Jack and Bowers took photos. But the men were in bad spirits. They were also worn out by the long climb.

Bowers

Captain Scott

Evans

Oates

Wilson

Meanwhile, Amundsen was just one week from base camp. His men were moving fast.

I'm starting to enjoy this!

Scott's party headed back but it was hit by blizzards again.

Things went from bad to worse. Evans got frostbite. Wilson was limping, then Scott hurt himself in a fall.

On 7 February they headed down the glacier. The men were getting weaker and weaker. Scott and Bowers discussed the shortage of biscuits.

I don't understand the shortage.

Perhaps the returning party took too many by mistake?

Where is Evans?

He's dropped back. I think he's over there.

On 11 February Scott took a wrong turn and got lost for two days. He couldn't find the depot in the fog. They were running out of food.

THey found Evans, on his knees with a wild look in his eyes.

Are you all right?

The men put Evans on a sledge and carried him to the next camp. But he died at midnight.

Can't... go... on.

Meanwhile, Amundsen and his team returned to base camp on 25 January, 1912. It was 99 days and 3,000 km after their departure.

Look, they're back already!

Any chance of a cup of coffee?

Back on the glacier, Scott and his men were in big trouble. They were running out of fuel to melt ice into water. There was a danger of dying of thirst. Scott was also getting ill from a lack of vitamin C.

It's nearly all gone! This is getting harder and harder.

Temperatures were down to -40°C. The ground was so rough that even the strong winds could not move the sails attached to the sledge.

How much longer can we keep this up?

At the next depot, the fuel had evaporated. The men were exhausted, frostbitten and trapped by the storm. They knew they were doomed.

Oates could no longer hide his pain. His toes were black with frostbite. On 16 March, Oates said he couldn't go on.

Don't give up. We'll get you back home.

The next morning, a blizzard howled outside...

I am just going outside and may be some time.

Oates bravely stumbled out of the tent. The others knew he was walking to his death. He was never seen again.

The blizzard raged on for another 10 days. Scott's last entry in his diary was on 29 March, 1912. Half-starved and nearly frozen to death, Scott wrote 12 letters before he died.

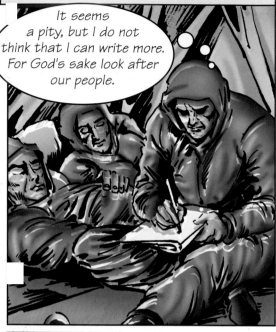

It seems a pity, but I do not think that I can write more. For God's sake look after our people.

FAST FACT The memory of Scott's heroic failure lives on in his letters and his diaries, reprinted many times since his death.

They were just 18 kilometres from the next food depot. If only they could have made it.

Eight months later, a search party found the frozen bodies of Scott, Bowers and Wilson. The tent was then collapsed over the bodies and a cairn was built to mark their grave. A pair of crossed skis was placed on top.

Poor devils!

It took Amundsen a month to make the voyage back to Tasmania. Amundsen desperately wanted to be the first to announce his victory in the race to the South Pole.

What happened to Scott?

On 7 March, 1912, Amundsen finally telegraphed his brother Leon with the news and it hit the newspapers.

AMUNDSEN REACHES S. POLE

A year later, in February 1913, the *Terra Nova* reached New Zealand. The news of Scott's death caused a sensation in Britain.
A service was held in St. Paul's Cathedral to mark his death.

A memorial fund was used to pay off the expedition's debts, provide for the dead men's families and set up the Scott Polar Research Institute, which is still going strong today.

Roald Amundsen had many other polar adventures, including flying over the North Pole in a hot air balloon in 1926. But the Poles would eventually claim his life, too. While on a rescue mission in 1928, Amundsen's plane crashed. He was never seen again.

When news of Scott's death was announced, people reacted more to Scott's tragic failure than to Amundsen's success. Amundsen's tactics of using skis and dogs were much better than Scott's motor sledges and ponies. However, Amundsen set out with just one aim: to reach the Pole first. An important part of Scott's expedition was to carry out scientific studies.

6 June 1868: *Robert Falcon Scott born in Devon, England.*

16 June 1872: *Roald Amundsen born at Borge near Christiania (Oslo).*

July 1881: *Scott joins Royal Navy.*

1888: *Nansen crosses Greenland from east to west.*

January 1898: *As part of* Belgica *expedition, Amundsen leads first skiing and sledging trips in Antarctica. Summer 1899 Scott meets Clements Markham and applies to lead expedition.*

May 1900: *Scott is appointed leader of Antarctic expedition.*

January 1902: *Scott sights Antarctica.*

December 1902: *Scott, Shackleton and Wilson reach a new farthest south.*

December 1906: *Amundsen in ship* Gjoa *becomes first to navigate the Northwest Passage.*

January 1909: *Shackleton's expedition turns back, just 180 km away from the South Pole.*

6 April 1909: *Robert Peary claims to have reached the North Pole.*

September 1909: *Scott announces second Antarctic expedition.*

9 September 1910: *Amundsen sends telegram to Scott to tell him he is heading for the South Pole.*

November 1910: Terra Nova *leaves New Zealand for Antarctica.*

4 January 1911: Terra Nova *reaches Cape Evans.*

19 October: *Amundsen's party sets out for South Pole.*

1 November 1911: *Scott's party sets out for the Pole.*

14 December 1911: *Amundsen's party reaches South Pole.*

16 December: *Amundsen's party hoists Norwegian flag at South Pole.*

17 January 1912: *Scott's party reaches South Pole.*

17 February 1912: *Evans dies.*

17 March 1912: *Oates dies.*

7 March 1912: *Amundsen's* Fram *sails into Tasmania to announce his victory.*

29 March 1912: *Probable date of death of Scott, Wilson and Bowers.*

14 January 1913: *Memorial service for Scot and his companions in St Paul's Cathedral.*

6 November 1913: *Scott's journals are published.*

18 June 1928: *Amundsen dies somewhere in Arctic in plane crash.*

January 1957: *Amundsen-Scott South Pole station named after the two explorers.*

1 *In an Antarctic blizzard, snow is hurled at your body and the wind creates a deafening roar. The fine snow stings your eyes and fills your nose and ears. You can get lost just a few steps from your tent.*

2 *The Antarctic has most of the world's fresh water. But the water is trapped as ice. Scott and Amundsen had to melt the ice to make water. When Scott ran out of fuel, his men were in danger of dying of thirst.*

3 *Husky dogs are bred for living in the snow. Their thick hair keeps them warm. They just curl up tight and sleep in the snow.*

4 *The motor sledges that Scott took to the Antarctic each cost the same as 660 husky dogs! They could only travel at 3-4 km/h. They were heavy, too. One motor sledge broke through the ice as it was unloaded from the ship.*

5 *Antarctica is covered by an enormous sheet of ice. At its deepest point it is 4750 m thick. It is formed by snow falling year after year.*

6 *When the bodies of Scott and his party were found in 1912, 16kg of rocks were found by their tent. Among them were plant fossils showing the remains of lush forests covering the continent 250 million years ago.*

7. *Two rolls of film were also found in Scott's tent, frozen under the snow for eight months. Amazingly, the film survived and showed Scott and his team at the South Pole.*

8 *If you drop your glove in the Antarctic it may be blown away, so explorers sewed their gloves onto cords attached to a harness over their jackets.*

9 *Both Scott and Amundsen depended on pemmican, dried meat mixed with fat. They also took special biscuits that were very hard and often had to be soaked in hot cocoa.*

10 *Hoosh is the hot meal eaten on a sledging journey, a mix of pemmican, biscuit and ingredients such as horse, seal meat or chocolate.*

11 *Amundsen named one of the mountains in Antarctica after his housekeeper Betty. She had knitted woollen vests for all of his team!*

12 *There is only one river in Antarctica, called the Onyx. It flows for just a few weeks each summer.*

13 *The first explorers used reindeer fur sleeping bags. But reindeer hairs stuck in their nose and mouth and when the ice in their clothes melted, the bags became soggy, and smelly!*

Arctic: *A region around the Earth's North Pole. The Arctic includes parts of Russia, Alaska, Canada, Greenland and Norway, as well as the Arctic Ocean. The boundary is usually considered to be the Arctic Circle, which is the limit of the Midnight Sun.*

Antarctica: *The region around the South Pole. Unlike the Arctic, it is a solid continent, but it is almost entirely covered in ice. It is the coldest place on Earth.*

Blizzard: *A severe snowstorm caused by winds moving at over 55km/h.*

Crevasse: *A deep crack in a glacier. Crevasses are often covered in snow and so are difficult to see.*

Depot: *A cache of food and fuel.*

Evaporate: *When a liquid changes to a vapour and rises into the atmosphere.*

Expedition: *A journey undertaken by a group of people with a set objective, such as the exploration of new lands.*

Frostbite: *Damage to the skin and body tissues caused by extreme cold. Frost-bitten fingers and toes are white, cold and numb. Gradually they turn red and swollen and finally black. If the tissue dies, the injured part must be cut off.*

Glacier: *A large river of ice that is formed on land and flows slowly downhill.*

Hoosh: *The name for a hot meal eaten on a sledging journey, usually a porridge-like mixture of pemmican, biscuit and other ingredients.*

Husky: *A breed of Arctic sledge dog used by Amundsen and Peary. Many explorers bought dogs in Greenland and Russia and shipped them to the Antarctic.*

Ice: *Ice is frozen water. Most of the ice in Antarctica is made of fallen snow which compresses over time, as it gets thicker and thicker.*

Ice floe: *Any piece of floating sea ice whose edges can be seen. It can be from a metre to several kilometres across.*

Iceberg: *A massive floating island of ice and snow that breaks away from a glacier or an ice shelf.*

Ice shelf: *A thick sheet of floating ice that forms on the polar coast, as the ice sheet or a glacier flows off the land into the sea. An ice shelf can extend hundreds of kilometres out to sea. Early explorers were awed by the white cliffs of the Ross Ice Shelf, which was called the "Barrier" because it blocked the way to the South Pole.*

Inuits: *The native peoples of the Arctic lands, once called Eskimos.*

Man-hauling: *Men pulling sledges on foot, without the help of dogs or ponies. In deep snow, this could be incredibly exhausting.*

Magnetic Poles: *The Earth's magnetic field has two poles, one in the North and one in the South. Compass needles all point to the North Magnetic Pole.*

Midnight Sun: *North of the Arctic Circle and south of the Antarctic Circle,* the Sun never sets in the summer months; it can seen for 24 hours a day.

Northwest Passage: *A sea route from the Atlantic to the Pacific through the Arctic Archipelago of northern Canada and along the northern coast of Alaska. Norwegian explorer Roald Amundsen led the first expedition across it between 1903–1906.*

Pack ice: *Pack ice is formed when the sea freezes. It may be a continuous sheet covering many square kilometres. Or it may be broken into many ice floes that can be closely packed together, or widely dispersed with channels of open water between them. Under pressure from winds and currents, pack ice can crush a ship.*

Pemmican: *Mix of dried beef, ground to a powder and beef fat. The idea of pemmican came from North American Indians who pounded up dried buffalo meat and mixed it to a paste with fat and berries.*

Plymouth: *A town in southwest England on Plymouth Sound, where the River Plym flows into the English Channel. A major port for hundreds of years, it was the point of departure for Scott , as well as for the fleet commanded by Sir Francis Drake who fought the Spanish Armada (1588).*

Scurvy: *A disease caused by deficiency of vitamin C, characterized by spongy and bleeding gums, bleeding under the skin, and extreme weakness.*

Sledge: *A vehicle mounted on low runners pulled by working animals, such as horses or dogs. Sledges are used for transporting loads across ice, snow, and rough ground.*

Snow blindness: *Damage to the eyes caused by the glare of reflected sunlight off snow. It is incredibly painful. Explorers hit by snow-blindness bandaged their eyes and were tied to a sledge so they would not get lost.*

Tent: *A shelter, usually made of canvas or skins stretched over a frame of poles, that can be easily carried. The special pyramid-shaped tent used by Arctic explorers was designed by an Englishman, Major Frederick Jackson, who took the idea from Inuit skin tents.*

Transantarctic Mountains: *The range of mountains that crosses the Antarctic continent and is one of the world's longest mountain chains. Amundsen and Scott saw different part of this range during their treks to the South Pole.*

Vitamin C: *A vitamin found naturally in plants, fruits and vegetables that prevents or treats scurvy.*

Volcano: *An opening in the Earth's crust from which molten lava, gas and ash erupt to the surface, sometimes forming mountains. In 1908 members of Shackleton's expedition were the first to climb Mount Erebus. Antarctica's most famous volcano.*

INDEX